A **5** Is Against the Law!

Social Boundaries: Straight Up!

**Funding for this book has been
provided through**
*PA Parents and Caregivers Resource
Network's*
**Mini Money Grant Program
(1-888-572-7368)**

---

*An honest guide for
teens and young adults*

Kari Dunn Buron

APC

Autism Asperger Publishing Co.
P.O. Box 23173
Shawnee Mission, Kansas 66283-0173
www.asperger.net

©2007 Autism Asperger Publishing Co.
P.O. Box 23173
Shawnee Mission, Kansas 66283-0173
www.asperger.net

Publisher's Cataloging-in-Publication

Buron, Kari Dunn.
    A 5 is against the law! : social boundaries : straight up! / Kari Dunn
Buron. -- 1st ed. -- Shawnee Mission, Kan. : Autism Asperger Pub.
Co., 2007.

        p. ; cm.

    ISBN-13: 978-1-931282-35-2
    ISBN-10: 1-931282-35-8
    LCCN: 2006935599
    "An honest guide for teens and young adults."
    Includes bibliography.

    1. Autistic youth--Behavior modification. 2. Autism in
adolescence. 3. Social interaction in youth. I. Title.

RC553.A88 B87 2007   2006935599
616.85/882--dc22   0611

This book is designed in Times New Roman and Helvetica Neue.

Printed in the United States of America.

*This book is dedicated to all the campers
who have ever attended
Camp Discovery at Courage North in
Lake George, Minnesota.
You have taught me so much.*

I would like to thank ...

I would like to thank my good friend Joyce Santo, who is always willing to help me work through good ideas. Friends like Joyce can help make good ideas even better!

I would also like to thank Anne Davis, who took the time to read the manuscript and help me choose the right words.

I want to thank my friend Paula Jacobsen, whose helpful suggestions continued to enrich the activities.

I want to thank my friend Sarah Attwood, who is an editor, an author and, best of all, a friend. Her suggestions helped me make things more universal.

Finally, I want to thank my editor, Kirsten, who really gets my thinking and is simply fun to work with.

Table of Contents

Who Will This Book Help?

- If you have ever gotten in trouble because of how you talked to someone or touched someone, this book might help.

- If you want to find friends and fit in socially but keep making mistakes that make that really hard, this book might help.

- If you have ever pursued a relationship and the object of your affections (the person you pursued) accused you of harassment, this book might help.

- If you just want to learn more about yourself and other people, this book might help.

Here Are Some Ways This Book Might Help You

1. It can teach you how to use a 5-point scale to help you learn about yourself and others.

2. It can help you understand that other people might think about behavior differently than you do.

3. It can give you examples of things that can accidentally get you in big trouble with the law.

4. It can explain how stress or feeling anxious can make it hard to think straight or make good decisions.

5. It can help you recognize situations that are hard for you and give you some good ideas about how to relax your body and mind when you face those situations.

6. It can help you use your strong, logical brain to better understand confusing (and sometimes stressful) social encounters.

What Is a 5-Point Scale?

The 5-point scale is a way to explain **your behavior** in a way that might help you understand it better. A 5-point scale takes an idea or behavior and breaks it into five parts to make it easier to understand the different *degrees* of behavior.

You can make a different scale for different behaviors. The scale we are going to focus on first is one that breaks down your behavior and visually illustrates how each level of behavior might make other people feel and what might happen as a result.

Check it out:

5 **Physically hurtful or threatening behavior.** These are behaviors that are against the law. For example, hitting someone or grabbing them in a private place. You will get fired from a job, suspended from school and maybe even go to jail if you engage in such behavior.

4 **Scary behavior.** This could include swearing or staring. You would probably get fired from a job for this behavior or suspended from school. This behavior could also end up being against the law.

3 **Odd behavior.** This behavior could make other people uncomfortable. It might include sitting too close to someone or putting your face too close to someone who wasn't expecting it. It could also include showing up at a party that you weren't invited to. You might get fired from a job because this behavior makes other people nervous. This is not against the law.

2 **Reasonable behavior.** This type of behavior is like going to a party you have been invited to and talking to someone you know. It might be playing a planned board game with someone, working with someone in a group at school or eating together at lunch. People are enjoying each other's company at this level. This is where people get to know each other better.

1 **Very informal social behavior.** This is like waving to someone or smiling to someone in the hallway at school. If you just say "Hi" and keep on walking, that is also a 1. This is totally O.K. and is the way most people first notice each other.

Once you learn about the levels of the scale, you can begin to rate your own behaviors. It is important to understand how you feel about each level and to find out how other people feel about each level. Believe it or not, some people have totally different ideas about behavior and levels than you do, and those people can influence what happens in the end. We will talk more about this later.

For the most part, bosses care about people getting along at their business. If too many people say that your behavior scares them, this could get you fired, even if *you did not mean to scare* anybody. I know this sounds unfair, but that is the way things work sometimes, so I suggest you learn about the scale and how your behavior fits the five levels.

Here's a sweet activity you can try with a little help from your parents, a teacher or a social skills group.

It might be a little frustrating to try to do this alone at this point. Fill in each number with the behaviors you think fit each level.

5 _____

4 _____

3 _____

2 _____

1 _____

When Does a 2 Become a 3, or a 4 Become a 5?

One of the interesting and sometimes confusing things about social behavior is that when you are young, you might do something that people consider a #2 behavior – that is, something that is perfectly acceptable. But then when you are a little older, that same behavior turns into a 3 – a little odd.

One example of this is a friend of mine (we'll call him Fred), who likes hair. He loves the way it feels and the way it smells. When Fred was in elementary school, he used to touch other students' hair. Sometimes, if he was behind someone waiting in line to go to recess or to get a drink of water, he would lean his head towards the person and smell his or her hair. People thought this was a little weird, but nobody was really afraid of him. Fred was just a little boy, so everyone thought the behavior was just a 3 (a little odd).

When Fred started middle school, he still liked to smell hair, so he would look for opportunities to get as close as possible to someone else's hair. One day, he put his face really close to a girl's hair, and she screamed! Not only that, she told the principal and her parents that Fred was harassing her by scaring her. The principal agreed that Fred's behavior, once considered a 3, had now become a 4 – truly scary and possibly against the law.

Behavior ratings can also change depending on who you are with. For example, another guy (we'll call him Carlos) was hanging out with some of the boys in his high school and noticed that they were all swearing. Carlos wanted to be popular so he said a few swear words, too. Nobody seemed to care; it seemed to Carlos that swearing was a 2 – reasonable, acceptable behavior – because nobody acted afraid and nobody thought it was odd.

Well, one day Carlos cussed in front of a teacher and was sent straight to the office. He was totally confused because he thought swearing in high school was O.K. The principal told him that it wasn't a 2 or even a 3; he said that swearing at teachers was a 4 – against the rules.

Once you understand the scale, you can ask your parents or teachers to help you revise the scale – depending on the situation, who you are with, or how old you are. It might be helpful to let your principal or boss know that you could use some help with this.

A good thinking activity: Think of something you used to do when you were younger that was a 2 then, but would be considered a 3 or even a 4 today.

Why do you think the rating changed?

Does the change seem reasonable?

What might this rating change mean to you now?

Different People See and *Think* About Things Differently

Another way to use the 5-point scale is to fill it out based on how you **think** about various behaviors and then have someone else fill it out to see if you agree or disagree.

It is very important to know how other people in your world *think* about your behaviors. For example, this girl I know (let's call her Alice) was fascinated with the way things taste. She always talked about how different things might taste. Sometimes she talked about more ordinary food combinations like peanut butter and chocolate; at other times, she talked about something more unusual, like cream poured over a hamburger.

Most people knew that Alice liked to talk about different flavors, so she didn't think this habit would be anything more than a 2 or maybe a 3. Then one day, in ancient history class, the teacher talked about a group of people who were known to be cannibals. Alice was fascinated – she hadn't thought about tasting a human being before. She now had a hard time *not* thinking about it, and even asked questions about how different human parts might taste.

Alice's teacher and her classmates were so upset by her questions that Alice was sent home from school. The principal told her parents that he did not think she could come back because she had scared her classmates and they no longer felt safe around her. Clearly, the others rated her behavior at a 4+.

This was a major difference of perspective! Alice thought she was asking a simple question (repetitive but simple), but everyone else thought she was actually thinking about tasting a real person.

See how what another person thinks can affect you and your future?

I'm going to give you one more example because this is really important stuff. I knew this guy (call him Joe) who was fascinated with Adolph Hitler. He was interested in the impact Hitler had on world history. Hitler became Joe's favorite topic to talk about. At first the other students thought the subject was a 3 (odd but not really scary). However, when Joe continued talking about it, they started to see it as a 4. They started thinking that if Joe was so fascinated with Hitler, maybe he approved of what Hitler did or even had plans to emulate him. This wasn't true, but it was how they started to *think* about what Joe was doing. Soon they quit talking to Joe.

Another good activity: Here are two scales.

1. Find a partner (a parent, teacher or a friend). Together, make a list of different behaviors (like staring at someone, sitting near someone, swearing at someone, or just saying "Hi" to someone). Be sure to include any behaviors that have gotten you into trouble.

2. Now both of you fill out a scale using those behaviors (do this separately, no peeking). Fill in where you think each of the behaviors belongs and where you *think* the other person will put the same behavior.

3. Now compare your scales. Do you both think the same about the different behaviors?

Number	Your Thoughts	Your Guess About Someone Else's Thoughts
5		
4		
3		
2		
1		

Number	Your Thoughts	Your Guess About Someone Else's Thoughts
5		
4		
3		
2		
1		

Nobody Goes It Alone

It is important for you to know that nobody is perfect at figuring out other people's perspectives. We all make social mistakes once in a while that are totally an accident. One example is if you misjudge a situation. Or perhaps the conversation is going so fast that you don't think through some of the things you say, and "Bam!" before you know it, you have hurt someone's feelings or made somebody mad.

The thing to remember when this happens is that you can repair the mistake.

As soon as you realize that something has gone wrong, or when someone's face begins to look irritated and you don't know why, you can ask, "Did I say or do something wrong?" If the answer is yes, then say, "I'm sorry."

People say they are sorry to help smooth out the rough spots in social interaction. Even if you did not mean to upset someone, saying you are sorry is usually the quickest way to make things better.

Another way to repair a mistake is to ask a friend or a trusted person if he or she thinks you made a mistake. Most people do this a lot because it is hard to learn from our mistakes if we don't know what they are.

Asking someone who cares about us is a good way to learn about ourselves, how our voice sounds and how we are doing with our body language (the messages we send to others depending on our gestures, how close we stand or how our face looks).

A good activity to do with a friend: Ask a friend or someone you trust about your body language, your voice tone, and your facial expressions. Do they think that you always say what you want to say with your body? For example, sometimes when we talk to other people, we sound angrier than we really are and the person might ask, "Are you mad at me?"

That is a pretty obvious example. In other cases, the other person might not ask if you are mad but might *think* it and you will never know.

Some things to talk about are:
- How your voice usually sounds
- How your face looks
- Where your eyes are focused when you are talking to someone
- What your arms are doing when you are explaining something
- How close your face is to the other person when you are trying to get a point across

It is very hard for you to know about this unless someone you trust tells you about it.

When a Kiss or a Glance Becomes a Crime

Another Example of How a 2 Behavior Can Become a 5

A *social boundary blunder* is when you get too close to someone, look too long at someone or touch someone in a way that he or she finds uncomfortable. In other words, stepping over their social boundaries. It is an accidental thing. A blunder means you did not mean it to be "inappropriate" or offensive.

Understanding social boundaries is important, because you can get into trouble, or unintentionally lose a friend, if you get it wrong.

Social boundaries change as you grow older. A child can look at someone for such a long time that the other person might think he is staring, and his mom might have to tell him that it is not polite to stare. Nothing serious; in other words, kind of like a 3.

But if a 16-year-old boy looks too long, the other person (especially a girl or woman) might think he is *"leering"* or that he is thinking about doing something harmful, and therefore find the behavior threatening and scary (like a 5). In fact, a lot of things that are considered "impolite behaviors" when you are young can become "threatening behaviors" when you are older, because social boundaries are being broken.

Social boundaries are very confusing because there are many unwritten social rules – also called the hidden curriculum – about dating and having girlfriends or boyfriends. If a girl and boy really like each other and ***they have both discussed this and decided together*** that they feel the same way, then kissing is usually thought to be a 2 (in private) or a 3 (in public). However, if a high school boy kisses a girl who has not agreed that she likes him, kissing becomes a crime and is against the law! No kidding, the girl can press charges. It is totally against the law.

Try this!
With a parent, teacher or friend, list Level 1 and Level 2 social behaviors. These are behaviors that you can look for to help you know that another person is still happy with you.

Level 1	Level 2

Here is a bonus activity for social skills groups – this is social thinking practice.

There is a book called *The Hidden Curriculum* (Myles, Trautman & Schelvan; www.asperger.net). In fact, there's even a one-a-day calendar with hidden curriculum ideas (www.asperger.net). Both are about how important it is to learn the *little details* of social behavior and social boundaries. Staring too long at someone is one of those details. Not swearing in front of teachers or your boss would be another one of those details.

If your teacher has the book or calendar about the hidden curriculum, you can look through it for ideas; otherwise, you can do this with the whole group and compare.

Think of rude behaviors and behaviors that are against the law. Make two lists:

Rude or Annoying (3)	These Are Against the Law (5)

Understanding the Gray Areas

Some people can get really stressed about social interactions and social boundaries. Often they get stressed because they are afraid of making a mistake. This is probably a survival instinct because social interactions can get people into trouble if they don't learn as much as they can about society's unwritten rules. This is sometimes called the "hidden curriculum" because even though we need to learn it, we usually don't talk about it.

Some people understand social interactions faster than others. This is just like some people learning math or reading more quickly than others. Everyone is different, and social interaction can be a strength or it can be something you struggle with. Understanding social boundaries may be so hard that a person will need to have her own crisis plan. The 5-point scale can help with this.

For example, I know a young man, Robert, who thought a lot about kissing a girl he thought was pretty. Robert is a "black-and-white" thinker and, let's face it, romance is definitely a "gray" area, so it is not surprising that he ran into problems.

Robert thought that all he needed to do was to pick out a girl he liked and she would automatically be his girlfriend. He noticed that boys and girls kissed in the hallways of his high school. He didn't know that there was a whole process behind getting a girlfriend, and that there were many steps before kissing.

Robert also noticed that sometimes boys said things to their girlfriends about their bodies. He even noticed that teenage boys did this on TV shows and in movies. These were popular boys, not criminals or hoodlums. So one day Robert followed a girl he liked because he wanted her to be his girlfriend. When she looked at him, he told her she had a nice body. This scared the girl because she thought it was threatening behavior (a 5!), and she reported Robert to the school liaison police officer. The police officer told Robert that he was "walking a thin line" and that if he didn't straighten up, he would find himself in deep trouble.

Well, by this time Robert was *completely confused*. He had no idea that what he had done was wrong and he did not know what he should have done instead! Clearly, he was in trouble, but how could he make things better if he didn't have all the information?

It would have been really helpful if the police officer and Robert had known about the 5-point scale. Together with an educational support person, they could have illustrated how Robert's behavior became a 5 when he scared the girl. The girl did not know what was going on in Robert's head and, therefore, couldn't know for sure if she was safe or in danger. Robert's teacher or parent could have helped him understand what some #2 behaviors were that would be safe and that might even help him find a girlfriend.

Activity: Here is an example of how Robert's scale might look. This is a good thing to discuss with your parents or teacher, or in a small social skills group.

5 **Against the law.** Making comments about a girl's body. This can scare the girl and make her think you are dangerous. Also, never kiss or touch a girl unless she tells you it is O.K.

4 **Going out of your way to follow a girl in the hallway.** Some people might think this is too close to stalking behavior, which is against the law and scary.

3 **Staring at a girl that you like without ever talking to her.** This can look very strange and might make the girl not want to be around you. Remember: She cannot read your mind, so you must use words if you are going to look at her for more than just a second. Remember also to look at her face. If her face looks upset, then stop looking.

2 **Talking to a safe person about the girl you like.** Eating lunch at the same table as a girl you like. Working in a small group together. Sitting next to someone in an after-school activity club.

1 **Just looking at the girl you like briefly and smiling.** You can say "Hi" if you see her outside of school.

When Things Seem to Get out of Control

No matter how hard we try, there are times when we get upset, anxious or even lose control as we go about our daily lives at school, at work or even at home. We are now going to look at another scale; in fact, it is a specially designed curve that can help you understand about your own level of anxiety. Once you understand your own anxiety curve, you can use it to explain yourself to your parents or to a special teacher.

This scale is a little different from the first scale we talked about. The ratings are all about feeling nervous, stressed and anxious. This is how it works.

You are at a **1** when everything is just fine. You are relaxed and happy. This is when you are best able to learn and meet people. ***People are not usually scary to others when their bodies and faces are at a 1.***

When you are at a **2,** you are feeling a little nervous. This isn't bad, but it might mean that you are a little uneasy about something or that you are uncomfortable for some reason. Most people can still work and think when they are at a 2. Most people are not scary when they are at a

2, but it is important to identify what things might make you feel like a 2. Maybe you feel this way when a room is too hot or too cold. Maybe you feel like this when you are hungry or when you are a little grumpy. Some words that describe a 2 are *crabby, irritable,* or *moody*. **It is important to have some ideas about what will help when you feel like a 2.**

When you are at a **3,** you are really starting to get nervous. A lot of things can make us feel nervous. Being told you did an assignment wrong or feeling like people are ignoring you are both examples. You might feel like a 3 if a talk with a friend goes bad or if you start feeling scared or stressed. You may feel really anxious or jumpy and you may start pacing. This is a very, very important feeling to be aware of. **If you are feeling like a 3, you should have a plan for how to calm your body**.

The main reason you want to be aware of your #3 feelings is that this is your last chance for clear and reasonable thinking. This is when you need to make an important decision that will seriously affect what happens next. That decision might be to take a walk, go to the counseling office, or talk to a safe adult. You should talk to a trusted adult about some good ideas to do at a 3.

This is a good time to do something relaxing, like looking at pictures of your favorite things, deep breathing, or listening to soothing music. Relaxing your face by massaging your jaw can help too, because sometimes a stressful face can look scary to other people.

When you are at a **4,** you are not thinking clearly! In fact, a famous man named Tony Attwood says that your IQ drops 90 points when you are at a 4. This is extreme stress or anger. Extreme anxiety can be something that builds up gradually or it can be caused by something that makes you go to a 4 really fast. This is the **Danger Zone**. It is one step away from breaking the law.

If you reach a 4, you need to have a bail-out plan, one that you have thought about in advance and that you have *practiced.*

- One of the best first steps is to **stop talking.** When people are at a 4, they are more likely to swear or raise their voice. #4 behavior is frightening to others. If you have a behavior program at school, you have probably gotten to a 4 a lot in your life.
- Another good idea when you are at a 4 is to put your hands together and try to keep them down and away from your face. When people are at a 4, they are more likely to swing their hands around. This looks scary and people might think you are about to attack them.
- Sometimes closing your eyes or putting your hands over your ears can help to calm your body.
- Learning how to slow down your breathing can also help.

The point is, you can't wait until you are at a 4 to figure this out. You have to have a **plan** for how to calm your body (check out some of the suggestions at the back of the book).

A hard truth is that if you reach a **5**, it is too late. You have already crossed a line that is likely to get you in trouble. This might look like a temper tantrum or a "meltdown." When you were young, you probably got in trouble, lost privileges or were sent to your room when this happened. Now that you are older, you might end up being at the mercy of the court if you engage in #5 behaviors!

After you have been to a 5, you will probably be pretty stressed out. It might take some time for your body to get back down to a 1. This is why you should have a plan for relaxing after things go wrong. You shouldn't try to go on with your day until you are sure you are all the way back down to a 1, or at least a 2. Give yourself time.

The Anxiety Curve: How to Use a 5-Point Scale to Teach Yourself and Others About Controlling Difficult Moments

This is what the anxiety curve looks like:

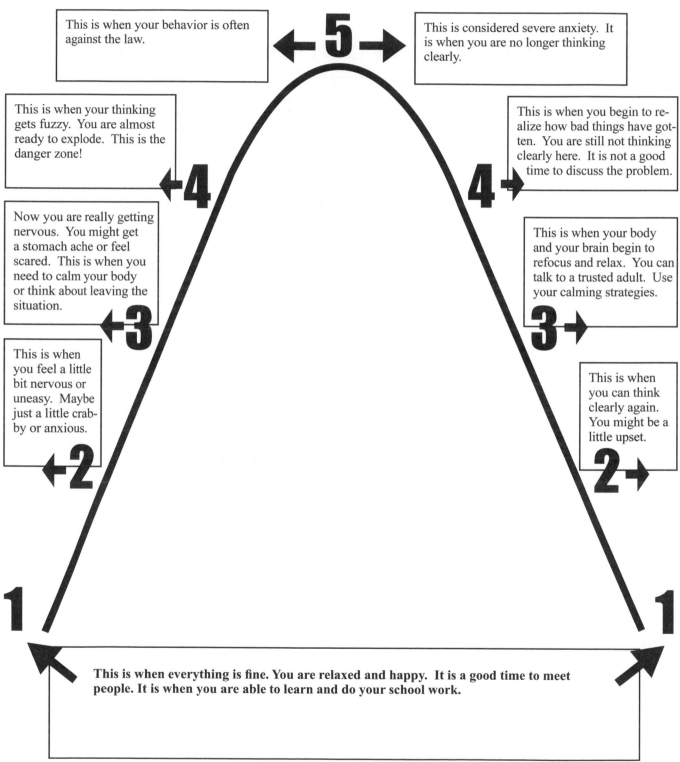

This is when your behavior is often against the law.

This is considered severe anxiety. It is when you are no longer thinking clearly.

This is when your thinking gets fuzzy. You are almost ready to explode. This is the danger zone!

This is when you begin to realize how bad things have gotten. You are still not thinking clearly here. It is not a good time to discuss the problem.

Now you are really getting nervous. You might get a stomach ache or feel scared. This is when you need to calm your body or think about leaving the situation.

This is when your body and your brain begin to refocus and relax. You can talk to a trusted adult. Use your calming strategies.

This is when you feel a little bit nervous or uneasy. Maybe just a little crabby or anxious.

This is when you can think clearly again. You might be a little upset.

This is when everything is fine. You are relaxed and happy. It is a good time to meet people. It is when you are able to learn and do your school work.

The Anxiety Curve; Buron and Curtis, 2004, *Proceedings manual.* ASA Conference, Seattle, WA. Used with permission.

Don't try to go back to work or to your classroom too soon because your brain and body may not be ready. Your IQ points are still low, so you might not make good decisions. Also, you might still be mad, and other people can't read your mind so they might still be afraid of you.

Don't chance it. Relax your body **first.** You don't want to lose control again. Close your eyes, stop talking, sit on your hands, run to the bathroom, do whatever you can to calm your body down.

Why It Is so Important to Control Your Anxiety and Anger

Knowing about your anxiety curve can make a huge difference in your life. There are some things you might not be able to do if you can't control your anger. For example, if you keep getting to a 4 or 5, you will not be able to get an apartment or live on your own, go to college and live in a dorm, or get a driver's license.

You will also have a better chance of being a part of a relationship or getting married if you can control your 4's and 5's. You will have a better chance of finding and keeping a job.

If you never learn to read, it is against the law for someone to discriminate against you. If you never learn math or science, you can still walk around your community independently. **But** if you can't learn to control your 4's and 5's, if you hurt or even scare other people, the community will not tolerate it, and you will lose your right to be an independent citizen.

It may sound severe, but having rules and laws like this is the only way our society can handle so many people living together without chaos. Some hard and fast lines must be drawn when it comes to hurting and scaring each other.

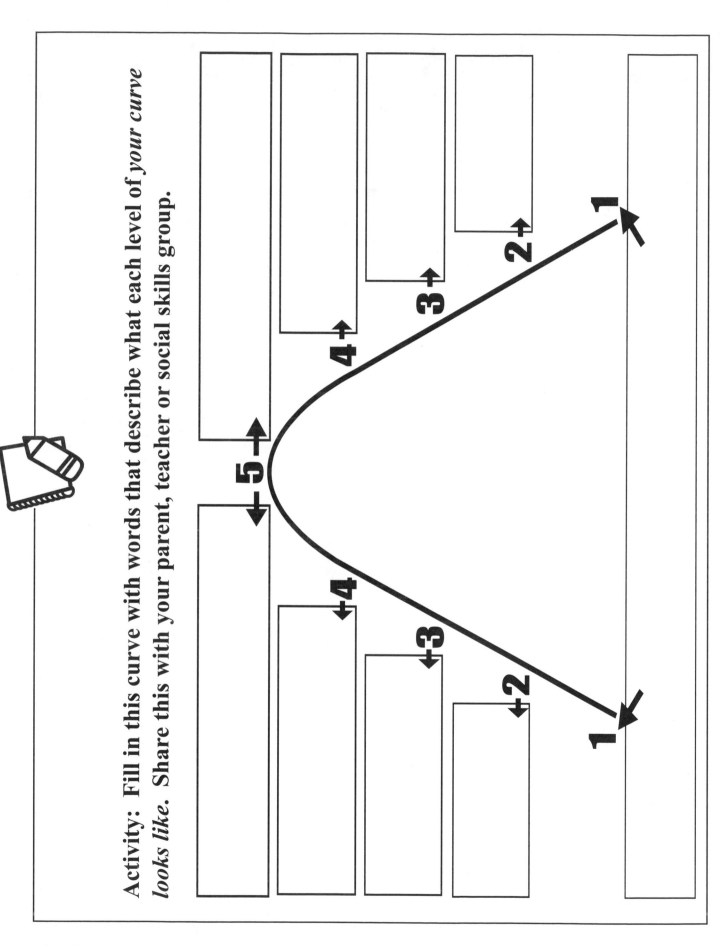

Activity: Fill in this curve with words that describe what each level of *your curve looks like.* Share this with your parent, teacher or social skills group.

Activity: Now fill in the curve with *things you can do* at each level to help prevent your anxiety from getting bigger. You may need some help from a parent, a teacher or a friend. This is a good way to share this information.

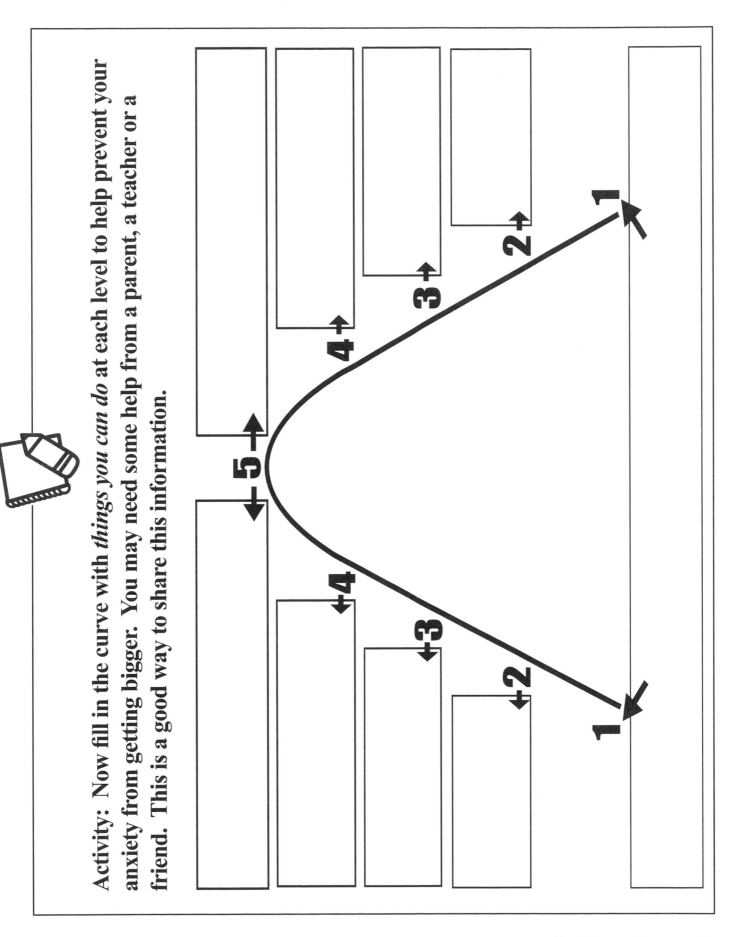

But It Isn't Fair!

This is the last thing I want to talk to you about. It has to do with another kind of crisis plan. This is a plan that is written just for you. I will tell you right up-front, you might not think the rules of this plan are fair. A famous scientist named Nancy Minshew calls these "never-ever rules." They are rules that *just have to be* in order for you and everyone around you to be safe. One reason you might not think your plan is fair is that other people might not have to follow the same kind of plan. It is totally understandable that you might be a little upset about this, so I will try to explain it the best I can.

Remember when I said that some people learn about social interactions really easily and other people don't? Well, if you are over 10 years old and you are still getting to a level 4 at school or at work, you need extra help to handle your behaviors and stay out of trouble. If you are trying really hard to get along with other people but things keep falling apart, then you also need extra help.

Social boundaries are very important, and it is so important that we don't get to a 5 that if the things we try first don't work, we have to get really serious. This plan is a serious life saver.

Another good reason to have a never-ever plan is that most social interactions go really fast, and this means you have to think really fast. The bottom line is that if social interactions make you kind of nervous, then stress will slow down your thinking. This can actually make it harder for you to think fast and keep track of what is going on.

O.K. – enough talk. This is what the all-important never-ever crisis plan is all about. It is about black-and-white thinking. Remember we talked about a lot of the social stuff being very "gray" and hard to understand? Your plan will be solid, clear, honest and systematic. In fact, it is a flow chart that you can follow like a map to get out of difficult situations.

Here is an example of one plan. My friend Taku wanted a date. He was over 21 years old and had a job. He was a nice, good-looking man and he enjoyed meeting girls. One day he met a really nice girl at work, Keesha. He talked to her, and she was very nice to him. That night he called her and asked her out for a date. Keesha said that she was busy and couldn't go. Taku thought this was a reasonable excuse, so he didn't get upset.

That weekend he called Keesha again and asked if she wanted to go out. She said that she had to do her laundry. Taku thought this was reasonable as well, so he didn't get upset. The next week Taku called Keesha five times. Each time he asked her out, and each time she had an excuse to say "no."

When Taku arrived at work the next week, his boss called him into his office and asked him why he was bothering his coworker, Keesha. Taku said that he hadn't bothered her; he was just asking her out on a date. The boss told him that his behavior was bordering on harassment and that if he did not stop, he would be fired!

The problem seemed to be that Taku did not recognize the girl's **nonverbal communication** (this is that gray stuff we talked about). That is, he did not notice that without saying so directly, she was not talking to him at work and she was not eager to go out with him. Taku did not understand that these two things meant that she did not want to go out with him at all and that he should stop asking.

People sometimes use gray communication when they don't want to hurt someone's feelings. That is, they make up an excuse so that their words sound kinder, but their **nonverbal** communication is saying, "I'm not interested."

Taku had not meant to upset the girl, and he certainly didn't think he would upset her so much that she would complain to the boss. But the reality was that he had upset her, mostly because he had a hard time reading that gray communication. Taku worked with his guidance counselor on a plan for making social decisions about calling girls. Taku's plan was called "Three Strikes and You're Out." This was a black-and-white, clear-and-simple, honest plan to help keep him out of trouble.

Taku's "Three Strikes and You Are Out" Plan

Taku meets a girl that he likes and who seems to like him, too. *He pays close attention to how she acts.* Is she smiling at him? Does she act like she wants to talk to him by staying near him and listening with her whole body? If he thinks she might like him based on both her verbal and nonverbal communication, he asks her out. If she says yes, great. If she says no, then *Taku must first talk about the situation with a trusted friend.* If the friend thinks it is O.K., Taku can ask her out again on another day.

If the girl says no a second time, Taku must wait until he sees her again at work or wherever they tend to see each other. *He will need*

---

to pay special attention to how she acts when he sees her again. Is she still smiling at him and standing near him when he is talking to her? Is she paying full attention to what he is saying?

These gray communication areas are critical because they help Taku understand if the girl is upset about his phone calls. If she doesn't want to talk to him or if she is no longer smiling at him, Taku must stop calling. These behaviors mean the same as spoken words, even if they are difficult to catch at times. Her behavior probably means that she is starting to feel uncomfortable around him.

On the other hand, if Taku sees that the girl is still smiling at him and acting in a friendly way, then he can ask her out *one more time.* If she says no the third time, then that is it! Taku should not ask her out again.

Some people might say that it is not a fair plan. What if the girl really did have to do laundry three nights in a row? What if she will say yes on the fourth try?

The statistics say that if a person says no to a date request three times, he or she will probably never say yes. We don't know for sure about every person, but we do know that Taku has a hard time "reading" that nonverbal gray talk. We also know that he almost got fired because of it.

This is Taku's *dating survival plan.* It will help him to feel safe about asking girls out. He won't have to worry that he might be scaring someone by accident. It is really kind of a safety plan. It will help Taku keep his dating behavior at a 1 or a 2. It isn't the whole answer, but it can make life simpler.

Taku's Flow Chart

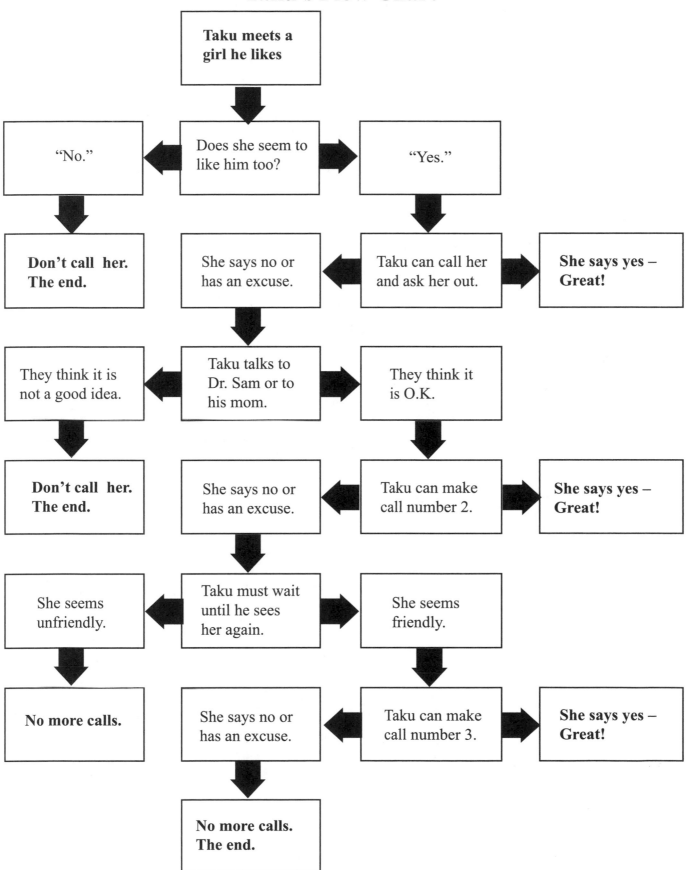

Last Words

It is not always easy to understand other people. Guessing how another person is going to feel about something you do can be very confusing. Sometimes it might seem like everybody knows what is going on but you! That is why I wrote this book. I tried to be very honest about how sometimes things just don't work out the way we expected. I tried to come up with some activities that might help you understand other people and yourself a little better. I hope it works, but if you try all of this and you still find yourself in trouble, **find help**. Talk to someone you trust and let them help you to figure out a plan that works for you. It is way too hard to do this on your own and it is way too important for you to do nothing.

Kari

Ideas for Keeping Your Body Calm or for Pulling Yourself down from a 4 to a 2, or from a 3 to a 1

- **Try organized relaxation classes at least two times a week.**
  This can be done as a part of your school program, at home or
  at a YMCA. The idea is to learn ways to help your body stay at
  a lower level all the time. Yoga and some of the martial arts are
  perfect ideas for this.

- **Learn about breathing.** Breathing can become very shallow
  when we are upset, and this makes it harder to calm down. When
  you are feeling upset, *slow your breathing down*. Take deep
  breaths and think about pulling the air from your feet all the way
  up and out the top of your head.

- **Put a small photo album together with pictures of things that make you feel good and calm**. Keep the photo album in your desk, in your purse or in a briefcase. If you are having a rough day, find a quiet place to sit and look at the photos. If you have a favorite place like a summer cabin, a boat or even a back yard swing, take a picture of it and put it in your photo album. When you look at the picture of a favorite place, close your eyes and think about being there.

- **Try a calming sequence.** A calming sequence is a short series of relaxing actions that you can practice many times throughout the day. If you do this routine enough, you will be able to use it in a crisis to help you calm your body and your brain.

- **Listen to calming music.** There are many kinds of music designed to relax and calm listeners such as nature sounds.

Activity: Try this calming sequence. Does it feels good and calming? How can you change it so that it works for you?

This calming sequence goes like this: Squeeze your hands together; close your eyes and rub your head; then rub your legs. Repeat the sequence five times, bringing your stress down.

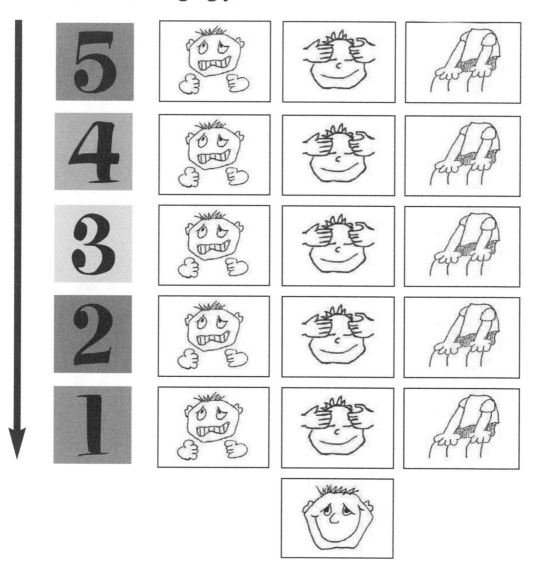

Resources

The Autism Society of Minnesota, www.ausm.org

Buron, K. D., & Curtis, M. (2004). *The incredible 5-point scale.* Shawnee Mission, KS: Autism Asperger Publishing Company.

Buron, K. (2006). *When my worries get too big!* Shawnee Mission, KS: Autism Asperger Publishing Company.

Myles, B. S., Trautman, K. L., & Schelvan, R. L. (2004). *The hidden curriculum. Practical solutions for understanding unstated rules in social situations.* Shawnee Mission, KS: Autism Asperger Publishing Company.

Myles, B. S. (2006). *The hidden curriculum – 2007 one-a-day calendar.* Shawnee Mission, KS: Autism Asperger Publishing Company.

APC

Autism Asperger Publishing Co.
P.O. Box 23173
Shawnee Mission, Kansas 66283-0173
www.asperger.net